COVER MODEL
JESSICA CRIBBON
All Hail Australia!

TABLE OF CONTENTS

Fashion and Style
Our fashion gurus offer up summer office and special events style tips. Hint: blue is in.

Sex and Dating
The Art of the BBQ Pick-Up is a lot easier than you think. Follow this blueprint and you'll be grilling to a bevy of beauties.

Kandy Koncierge
Throw these beauties on the grill and the BBQ pick-up will be a lot easier.

**SUMMER KRUSH
CHRISTINA RIORDAN**
Christina is California born and raised. The NORCAL beauty now calls SOCAL home and is our Summer Krush.

**KANDYSTAND SWEETS
CHELSEA NICOLE AND MELISSA CEJA**
SOCAL is representing this Summer in KANDY. Chelsea stuns in her itsy bitsy bikini and Melissa pops in her underwear.

KANDY MAGAZINE

LETTER FROM THE EDITOR

Hello readers! We unlocked our Kandy vault for another bevy of Kandy beauties. One of the sweetest Kandy girls to grace our pages, Christina Riordan is herein. We give you her Krush of the Month pictorial and interview in an itsy, bitsy tiny bikini. We have an amazing catalog of Cover girl Jessica Cribbon that we will publishing in the coming months.

The Kandystand is open for business. Chelsea Nicole Eyler and Melissa Ceja share with us their favorite Summer feature. We caught up past Kandy cover girl Elizabeth Deo and she shared her Summer Checklist.

We wrap up our lineup of Kandy sweeties downunder where it is now Winter. Say hello to Shona Child.

Thirsty for some Kandy knowledge? We stand ready to deliver with articles to brighten your day. Inside we have Summer fashion tips, summer grilling suggestions, summer fitness, and of course summer dating ideas.

Cheers!

Ron Kuchler
Editor in Chief

Editor in Chief
Ron Kuchler

Deputy Editor **Managing Editor** **Associate Editor**
Steve Scala David Packo Bill Nychay

Cover Photo by
Aaron Riveroll

Contributing Photographers
Aaron Riveroll, Guy Tadman, Mike Prado

Stock Imagery
Shutterstock, Fotolia, Adobe Stock

Contributing Writers
William Poole, Jim DeBellis, John Zakour, Javier Morales, Paul Cook

CONTACT US
Kandy Enterprises LLC
7260 W. Azure Dr Suite 140-639
Las Vegas, NV 89130
www.kandymag.com
www.facebook.com/kandymagazine
X @kandy_magazine
Instagram.com/kandymagazine

General Inquiries - info@kandymag.com
Public Relations - pr@kandymag.com
Letters to The Editor - letters@kandymag.com
Copyright - legal@kandymag.com
Model Inquiries - kandymag.com/become-a-kandy-girl
Photographer Inquiries - kandymag.com/helpout
Writer Inquiries - kandymag.com/helpout
Subscription Inquiries - kandy@kandymag.com

SUMMER 2024
© 2024 Kandy Enterprises LLC.
All Rights Reserved.

CHELSEA
NICOLE EYLER

Chelsea's Hometown:
Riverside, CA

Measurements: 34-26-34
Height: 5' 5"
Weight: 110 lbs
Hair color: Dark Brown
Eye color: Green

The best part of Summer is tanning on the beach, and the pool parties of course!!

Photos by: Aaron Riveroll

KANDYSTAND SWEETS

KANDY MAGAZINE

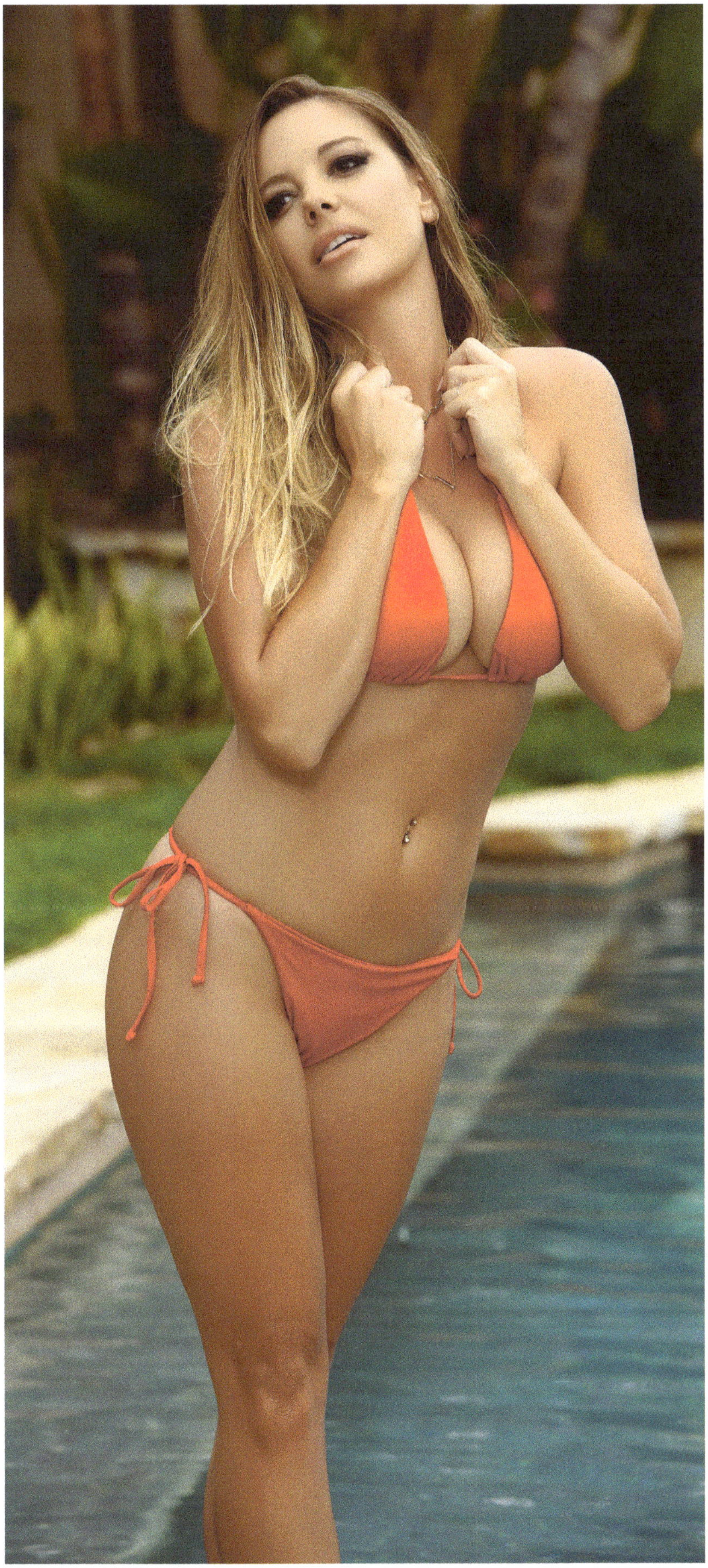

Kandy MAGAZINE

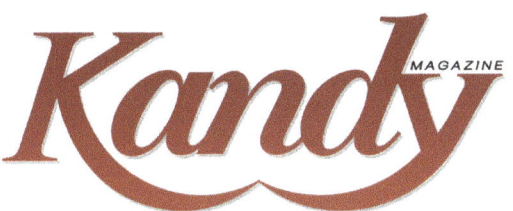

Make payment out to and Mail to:
Kandy Enterprises
7260 W Azure Dr. Ste 140-639
Las Vegas, NV 89130

Yes! I want KANDY! SEND ME:

6 issues for $54 (1 year)
12 issues for $96 (2 Years)
18 issues for $126 (3 Years)

____
First Name

____
Last Name

____
Street Address

____
Street Address

____
City

____
State

____
Zip Code

Remember Payment Enclosed
Please allow 6 to 8 weeks for delivery of first issue.
For Credit card payment options
www.kandy.store

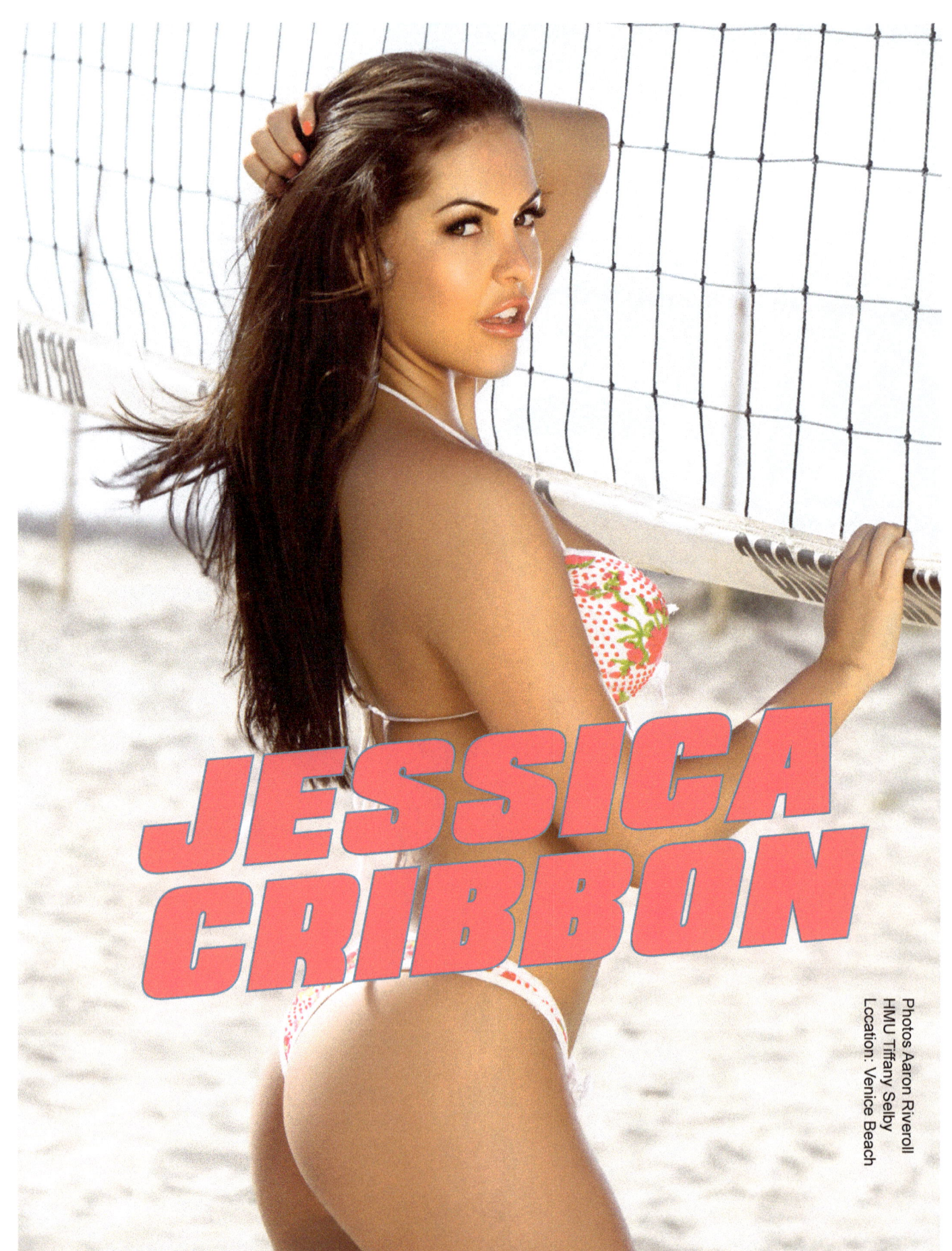

Photography by
Mario Barberio

Hair & MUA
Michelle Vanderhule

Christina Riordan
Krush of the Month

KRUSH OF THE MONTH

Our Krush of the Month is California born and raised. The NORCAL beauty, who know calls SOCAL home, attended college at California Polytechnic State University in San Luis Obispo, which is known for its engineering programs, where she obtained her Bachelor's Degree in Nutrition with a minor in Psychology. Like any good California Kandy girl, she loves modeling, fashion, California's beautiful beaches, traveling, fitness and is into Crossfit, nutrition, healthy living, and cooking. To use Christina's own words, "she is a California girl, and they know how to party!" So, what do you say we get this party started and get to know our July Krush of the Month a little bit better.

Christina, let's dive right into what our readers want to know about your personal life. Men. What has been the most creative thing a guy has done to get your attention? Hmmm....the most creative thing a guy has done to get my attention... I'm not too sure! Guys aren't too creative, I guess. Haha. I don't know! I think over the years I've seen and heard most pickup lines, or since I do a lot of racing events, I heard most guys try to rev their engines. Ha-ha. I think someone who makes me genuinely laugh is going to catch my attention more than someone trying to be flashy, even though I do like nice cars.

If we were to ask your best friend to pick out the perfect guy for you, how would she describe him? My best friend would describe a perfect guy for me as someone who is athletic and outgoing since I'm always active or working out or wanting to travel. A great sense of humor, because I always love positive energy and to laugh. Someone who is compassionate and trustworthy because you always need that! Gorgeous eyes and a nice smile don't hurt either.

Describe for us the ultimate 3rd date. For the ultimate third date, I think it would involve doing something active, yet romantic. Something like going for a little day trip either along the coast to the beach or for a sail on the water with a bottle of wine. An amazing view of the ocean - sun, fresh air, and wine...perfect!

Christina Takes Over Los Angeles

What do you miss most about your hometown? I think I miss my family the most from my hometown. I've always been close to them so not always getting the chance to see them or be with them on certain holidays or occasions.

What do you enjoy most about living in LA? I think the best thing about LA is that everyone is so active and full of life. There is always something happening, and I love how almost everyone is into healthy living. That is such a huge part of my life.

What has been the biggest adjustment to LA life? I think trying to find my way around all of LA and its traffic has been the biggest adjustment!

Any pet peeves on LA life? Traffic? Great pretenders? Catty models? My biggest pet peeve of LA is the horrible traffic and drivers. Haha. Other than that, in my modeling and talent industry there is always going to be catty models and pretentious people, but that's anywhere.

Tell us about one of your unusual modeling gigs. Oh man, I have had so many unusual modeling gigs over the years. Both good and bad. Since I do such a variety of modeling, I'm always doing something new. Amongst my many jobs, I've been a podium and an umbrella girl for many years. I have had the privilege to meet a ton of professional racers and celebrities. Being able to see behind the scenes of what it takes to go out there on the track and be a part of the excitement is amazing. I've met so many top world athletes over the years and continue to do so. I love it. I've enjoyed it so much it has inspired me wanting to learn how to ride a motorcycle and even take driving lessons to drive exotic cars around the track.

We saw you worked with Bret Michaels. Tell us about that experience. Yes! Working with Bret and the production team was so fun. He has such a great heart and was always so supportive and encouraging during filming. I guess being a busty blonde probably didn't hurt, ha-ha, but he was awesome. If you've seen the music video, "Girls on Bars", the whole shoot was like a big party. Lots of laughs and dancing. It was definitely fun times.

Christina Goes on the Road

Where are your 3 favorite places in the US? I haven't gone everywhere in the U.S., but I do love San Luis Obispo quite a bit. Even though I did live there going to college; you are close to the beach and mountains, and even some amazing wineries. The people are nice and there is never any traffic! San Diego is also amazing. The wonderful warm beaches, fun people, and great nightlife. I am going to choose Hawaii as my third because it just speaks for itself how gorgeous it is! You can obviously tell I love being by the ocean.

Which city has the friendliest guys? So far, from my experience ... before going to Austin, TX recently I would say San Luis Obispo, CA because, like I said, everyone there is super nice. But Austin seems to have that southern charm and chivalry.

KRUSH OF THE MONTH

Where would you say are the wildest women? I would probably say Vegas is a wild place in general for men or women. It's where people let their inhibitions go and everyone is out for a party or mischief.

Where is the one place that you have not been to yet that you dream of visiting? Right now, I have been wanting to go to Spain. I've been to Europe, but there are so many countries and cities to visit and explore. I love traveling and experiencing new places and cultures. You have to experience the most out of life while you can!

When you travel what is the one thing you take with you regardless of where or how long a trip? Well, besides my phone being an obvious choice for capturing some amazing moments while traveling, I always take my workout shoes and outfit. Regardless where I go, I will be out exploring or working hard somewhere.

CHRISTINA ON NUTRITION & FITNESS

Share your 5 top nutrition tips.
My top five nutrition tips are definitely:
1) Drink lots of water! Our bodies are 75% water. We need it! If our bodies are properly hydrated our skin, digestion, and weight is much healthier.
2) Eat small meals every couple hours. This helps with metabolism and keeps us from over eating at any one given point.
3) Get enough protein. This very important for very active and fitness oriented people. Having 1.5-2x the amount of protein our bodies need helps build muscle to help repair and make us stronger.
4) Eat clean. Organic and natural foods help prevent us from eating toxins from foods that may have normally been processed or containing pesticides.
5) Reduce sugar intake. Our bodies are fueled from the sugar called glucose, but we only really need small amount each day. We can get our sugars naturally through eating fruits and grains.

What is the biggest sacrifice you've had to make to live a balanced, healthy life? I've lived pretty healthy the majority of my life, but sometimes being a nutritionist is a bit of a blessing and a curse. Haha. I think knowing almost everything about foods I eat prevents me from fully enjoying a piece of pizza or a decadent dessert. I'll go out to eat occasionally, but I pretty much always order "healthy".

KRUSH OF THE MONTH

When you are on the road, do you make it into the hotel gyms or do you take a run outside? When I am on the road, it's tough to stay on top of my intense workout routine. Most of the time very long days make it hard to get the energy or minutes to workout. I try and utilize the hotel gyms and sometimes I even can do workouts in the room like push-ups, sit-ups, squats, etc.

So, do you have cheat days and if you do, what is your ultimate cheat meal? I don't really have a full cheat day. I like to eat very clean most of the time, but I may indulge in a cheat meal or dessert every once in a while. I love carbs quite a bit so I try and stay away most of the time, but I do love Mexican food as a "cheat meal" and this usually include lots of chips and salsa. Yum!

Is your exercise regimen more free weight, machines, TRX or high-intensity cardio? My workout regimen has evolved quite a bit over the last five years. I am such an active person I'm down to try anything fitness related. I used to do 30 minutes of cardio followed by 30 minutes of free weights and abs in the gym for my "daily workout". Though for the past 2 years, I am a regular at my local CrossFit. I've never seen better results for my body. I lift a ton of weights; do gymnastic movements, and a ton of cardio. It's very intense, but I love challenging myself. Reminds me of being on a team sport in school. My whole body is much more toned, lean, and stronger! I love it. I also do hot yoga, hike, and play basketball for alternate fitness days.

Are you a gym rat or do you get most of your exercise done outside a gym? Like I mentioned earlier, I usually am in the gym but I do love the California sunshine! So, I often do go out for a hike or a walk on the beach.

KRUSH OF THE MONTH

KANDY MAGAZINE

Kandy
VAULT

KRUSH OF THE MONTH

KANDY MAGAZINE

Kandy Krush Ingredients

Name: Christina Riordan
Hometown: Marina del Rey, California
Birthday: March 25th
Measurements: 34DDD-27-36
Height: 5'9"
Weight: 120 lbs
Hair: Blonde
Eyes: Green
Occupation: Professional Model, Actress, Nutritionist
Instagram @christina_riordan

Favorite Color: Blue

Favorite Flower: Sunflower

Favorite Clothing: I love tight black pants because they go with everything or a sexy backless dress.

Favorite Feature on a Guy: I love light colored eyes and a nice smile.

Favorite Feature on Yourself: Even though I work-out a ton, I am always complimented on my eyes and smile as well.

Favorite Wine: 2010 Pinot Noir, Belle Glos from Clark and Telephone Vineyard.

Favorite Music: Anything with a good beat! I listen to every type of music. Why limit yourself? Whatever mood I'm in I adjust my station accordingly.

Favorite Work-out Tune: Anything fast paced. It generally is EDM because of the high energy.

Favorite Exercise: GHD sit-ups. They work your entire core and quads.

Favorite Vacation Spot: Europe!

Favorite Food: Japanese, because I love the freshness and healthiness.

Favorite Beverage: I love tea. One of my favorite flavors is chai tea because I love cinnamon.

Favorite Actor and Actress: Brad Pitt and Angelina Jolie. They are both badass and sexy as hell.

Favorite Movie: I love so many! I think for an overall well-rounded movie I would choose James Bond films, especially with Daniel Craig. The adventure, exotic locations, amazing cars and romance make them an all-around winner.

Favorite Song: California Love by 2pac because I am California girl and we know how to party!!

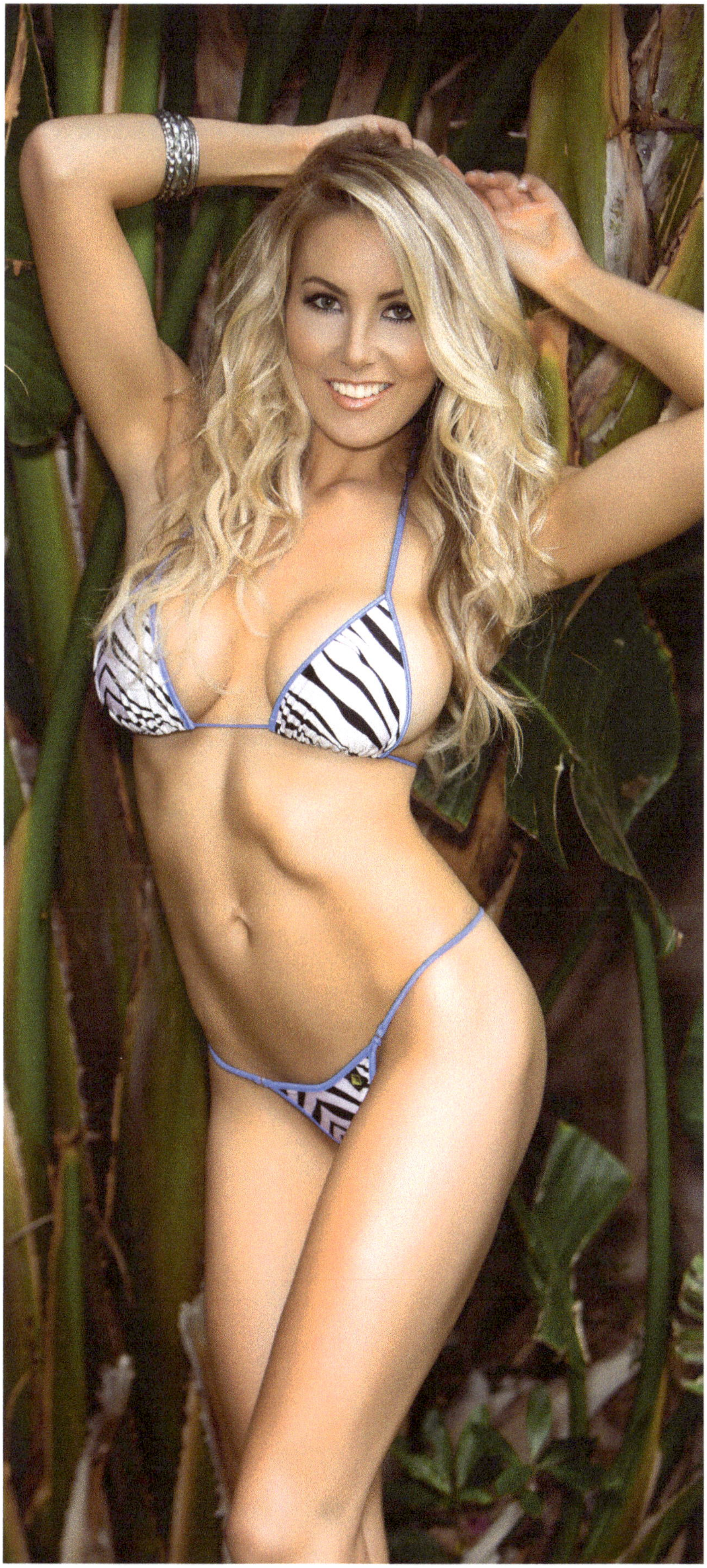

Kandy MAGAZINE

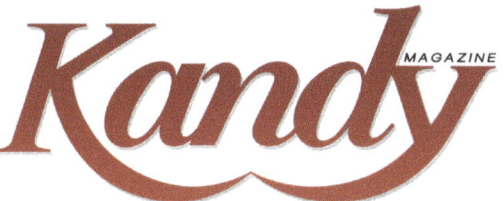

Make payment out to and Mail to:
Kandy Enterprises
7260 W Azure Dr. Ste 140-639
Las Vegas, NV 89130

Yes! I want KANDY! SEND ME:

6 issues for $54 (1 year)
12 issues for $96 (2 Years)
18 issues for $126 (3 Years)

____
First Name

____
Last Name

____
Street Address

____
Street Address

____
City

____
State

____
Zip Code

Remember Payment Enclosed
Please allow 6 to 8 weeks for delivery of first issue.
For Credit card payment options
www.kandy.store

KANDY SUMMER STYLE

MEN'S SUMMER STYLE

Credit: Viorel Sima Fotolia

→ What happens when you receive an invitation to attend a formal event or a wedding? Do you have a wardrobe packed with suits and formal apparel or do you have to run out to shop for a decent suit? Well, every man faces challenges when he is invited to an event. Not everyone has a perfect suit hanging in the closet. Therefore, you need to be aware of the latest formal fashion scene so that you can prepare for any unexpected or sudden event.

The good part about shopping for the summer season is that you get to have a lot of options. If you are one of those who don't keep up with the changing trends or find it hard to buy a thousand dollar suit, then you have to pick something that you can use for office, meetings, and other events as well. Let's not waste any more time and read onto the list of wardrobe essentials that you need to get your hands on to prepare to attend any event for the next two months.

Dress to Impress
Whenever you get an invitation to be part of a wedding or a corporate event, you have to dress in something that is not only unique but utterly impressive. Well, you heard it right. You cannot be boring and opt for old, traditional suits because the world is becoming more stylish by the minute. Runway fashion has definitely taken a turn in men's fashion. Therefore, we have quite a few trends in line for you for a perfect summer occasion. Anything too mainstream is not only going to make you look uninteresting but will also not prove to be lucky for you (yes, you will attract no girls). So, let's take a look at some of the hottest trends and formal fashion do's and don'ts for this year.

Matching Shirts & Trousers Days Are Over!
Remember the time when wearing same colored shirt and trouser was cool? Well, not anymore! Men's trends change quicker than the seasons. When you start to accept a new trend, you come to know that it is no longer in fashion. However, one thing is for sure, no matching shirts and trousers. If you really want to look trendy and on top of your fashion game at an event, you have to add more colors, textures, prints, and layers to your look.

Creating a Statement That Lasts
Statement pieces are very much in fashion, simply because they put you in the spotlight and who doesn't want to get attention? When wearing a suit, you can always go for a printed or colorful tie as a statement piece. If it is a wedding that you attend, you can replace the tie with a bow, but make sure that the bow is of any color but black.

When you want to create a style statement, you can go for a more interesting blazer or suit. A lightly printed black or blue suit will serve as a perfect statement piece and the good news is that printed blazers and suits are in fashion.

Checkered Suit for a Corporate Lunch

If a plain blue or black suit seems too mainstream, you can always go for playful options, especially in the summer season. Well, this is no surprise that patterned suits have been a great part of the runway fashion for summers, but if you missed the fashion news, here we have everything you need to know.

Adopting a unique style is never harmful. However, insure that the style is in trend and you have the attitude and budget to pull it off. A checkered suit or blazer is one piece that will do justice to your formal summer look. Whether you have to attend a corporate event or go on lunch with delegates, a checkered blazer will make you look flawless.

Tips to Wear a Checkered Blazer

It is best to buy a white colored blazer with blue checkered print. As it is the summer season, you may play with different colors as there are no limitations to the color you choose. A pair of light blue faded jeans paired with a white buttoned down shirt will complete the checkered jacket/blazer look. Now, you are all set to conquer any meeting or event with this flawless look.

Tie is No Longer a Necessity

If you always had trouble picking the best tie to go with your suit then there is good news for you. Ties are no longer a necessity for formal suits. You can opt for collar-less button down shirts and pair them with classy blazers to get a complete formal look. If you have to attend a semi-formal event, the best way to rock the tie-less look is to wear a button down checkered dress shirt with a dark blue blazer and a pair of khaki pants. You can go for a more corporate look by wearing a blue button down shirt with a pair of black dress pants and a grey blazer.

Flaunt a Classy Look

Off-white blazers and tuxedos are classy, sleek, and on point. Therefore, they are one of the most trending formal wears for this year. Hollywood men seem to love this style and have been seen pulling off an off-white tuxedo on different red carpet events. If you are thinking that you will only need to replace your blazer with an off-white one to get this look then you are sadly mistaken.

When wearing an off-white tuxedo, you have to make sure that your whole outfit is in sync with it. You can wear a black vest under your off-white jacket with a pair of black dress pants and a white dress shirt. To go for a slicker look, you can opt for white button down shirt and a pair of black pants to go with your off-white dinner jacket. It is best to wear a black bow tie with these looks.

The Red, White, and Blue Combination

There are many guys who want to make a unique appearance at any event that they attend. All they want is to turn heads and attract attention towards themselves. We have the look for such confident males; a combination of red, white, and blue suit. To create a preppy look, buy a red colored crisp coat, a pair of white twill trousers, and a light blue button down shirt. This is a perfect eye-catching look for a formal event, a corporate function, or just lunch with some colleagues.

Rich Colored Suit for a Night-Time Event

For a night-time event, buy a rich colored suit to be the events highlight. If you don't have a large budget to buy different suit types, get one neutral color suit and a rich emerald color suit to complete your wardrobe. Suits in rich jewel colors are perfect for corporate dinners and after evening functions. A rich emerald green suit will create a sophisticated look when paired with black colored bow tie and shoes.

Final Word

Summer season stands for weddings, outdoor events, and parties, and if you have a lot of invitations lined up, you have to be extra careful in picking the right apparel to look smart and fashionable at the same time. There are many other things that you need to take into consideration when preparing for a formal event or function. Accessories are one of the things that you can't miss, especially a good watch. It is always best to consider a pair of classic sunglasses for a daytime or evening outdoor event. Last but not least, make sure you carry yourself with confidence and nothing will keep you from becoming the center of attention. So, before you run out of time, hit the shopping mall and try out different suits and styles mentioned in this article. Keep in the mind the look you want to achieve, and then try out the best available options that come under your budget.

KANDYSTAND SWEETS

KANDY MAGAZINE

"I'm looking forward to wear little bikinis, working on my tan and expanding my acting experience this summer."

KANDY SEX & DATING

A Summer BBQ Is a Great Way to Get Things Cooking with That Hottie with the Body

By Jim DeBellis

→ Spring is for falling in love and winter is for making love. But summer is the time to party, have fun, and impress the girls with your masculine talents and abilities. Tender gazes in a breezy meadow of wildflowers are great, and so are those long passionate hours between the sheets on those cold winter nights – but nothing beats summer fun – playing volleyball on the beach, cruising in a vintage convertible, or getting the gang together in the backyard for a game of horseshoe and some ice cold beers.

And, of course, all that vigorous activity brings on those ravenous appetites for some great summer BBQ. That's where a man can shine. You might not be Betty Crocker in the kitchen, but every man needs to be a king of outdoor cooking. It's long been said that the way to a man's heart is though his stomach, but it's equally true that the way to a woman's heart (and some of her other prime real estate) is through cooking meat over a real fire in the great outdoors.

Whether it's your own party, a group get-together at a park or beach, or someone else's bash, a cookout always gives you an opportunity to be a take-charge man who will capture the attention of all the sweet young ladies. And a lot of guys and girls will be happy to let you light the coals or flip the meat if you're just visiting too.

Photo Credit: fotolia / Monkey Business

You'll need to focus on two things: great food and skillful but natural pick-up techniques.

The Food

Let's start with the food. You must have at least one specialty in outdoor cooking (and, no, it can't be hotdogs) and a secret recipe, technique, or a sauce with a secret ingredient.

Starting the fire

If starting a fire were as easy as twisting a knob or pushing a button, with no soot or ashes involved, women would just do it themselves – and plenty of them do it all the time anyway. But a BBQ gives her a chance to be a "girl" and you a chance to be a caveman. The ladies can bring the potato salad and the beans, and you can buy, bring, and cook the meat. If you're cooking with propane, no problem. It's still a mechanical device and a real flame, so a real man is needed. Just make sure you have plenty of gas, a clean grill, and know how to light it.

Hardwood charcoal is always better than briquettes, but the main thing is to get a nice hot bed of coals going. Five pounds of charcoal is enough for only about three pounds of meat so don't be stingy with the coals or the meat won't cook. If you don't have a starter chimney, pile the coals into a pyramid in an ash-free grill, soak them well with lighter fluid, then (and this is important) wait for three to five minutes, and then light them with a long match or fireplace lighter. If the flames don't singe your eyelashes, then you waited long enough. After about 30 minutes, spread them out and start cooking.

Cooking the meat

Steaks, chicken, chops, ribs, and burgers are always popular. Marinated meat is always a good idea for grilling to ensure you have a moist and properly seasoned entrée. If you are not an expert, ask someone who is or look on the Internet for cooking instructions for your selected meat, because it is important that you have the confidence to look like a Zen master at the grill. Using a meat thermometer is not only a good idea, it will make you look professional.

BBQ ribs, pulled pork, and other sauced delicacies are also popular. To save time at the grill, it is a good idea to bake ribs in the oven in a foil-covered baking pan at a low temperature (about 250 F) for a couple of hours before the party. This will get rid of a lot of the fat and allow them to cook to nicely in the same time it takes to cook raw chicken. Once they are done, you can sauce them and put them back in a covered baking pan with the grill closed (but top and bottom vents open) to soak in the sauce.

There are a lot of good jar sauces, but you always need to at least "doctor" it up to make it taste homemade. Caramelized onions, the juice of an orange, a drop or two of liquid smoke, and maybe a dash of hot sauce can make all the difference. BBQ is a sweet and sour sauce, so you can always add a splash of vinegar and/or brown sugar or honey to suit the local taste. Ketchup with brown sugar, vinegar, granulated garlic, sautéed onions or onion soup mix, a couple of large dollops of apricot preserves, and a small bottle of Russian dressing can also be used to create or dress up an ordinary BBQ sauce. Just don't tell them everything that's in it, because it's very mysterious and cool to have your own secret recipe.

Get the Girl

Okay…let's not forget about the reason for all of this preparation and hard work – getting the girl! The chef is like a deejay or the drummer in the band, especially if he is the one doling out the burgers or chicken legs or other delicious meat. You will get comments from curious ladies all throughout the cooking process when they hear the sizzle and smell the aroma – so take advantage of every big-eyed smile and every question about what's cooking and when it will be done. Find out about her, what she likes to cook, and if she can save you a seat at her table.

If you aren't the chef, a BBQ is still a great way to meet girls. If you see her pumping the keg without the tap open, explain to her that it will make the beer foamy. Then open the tap, let the foam run off, and fill her glass perfectly with just the right amount of head by pumping only when it's open.

Sometimes the best dating tips have nothing to do with your sexy moves and clever comments and everything to do with just letting her observe you being a guy. The summer BBQ is one of those great opportunities. And those outdoor cooking skills will serve you well right into the fall when you invite your new summer love to go tailgating with you before the big football game.

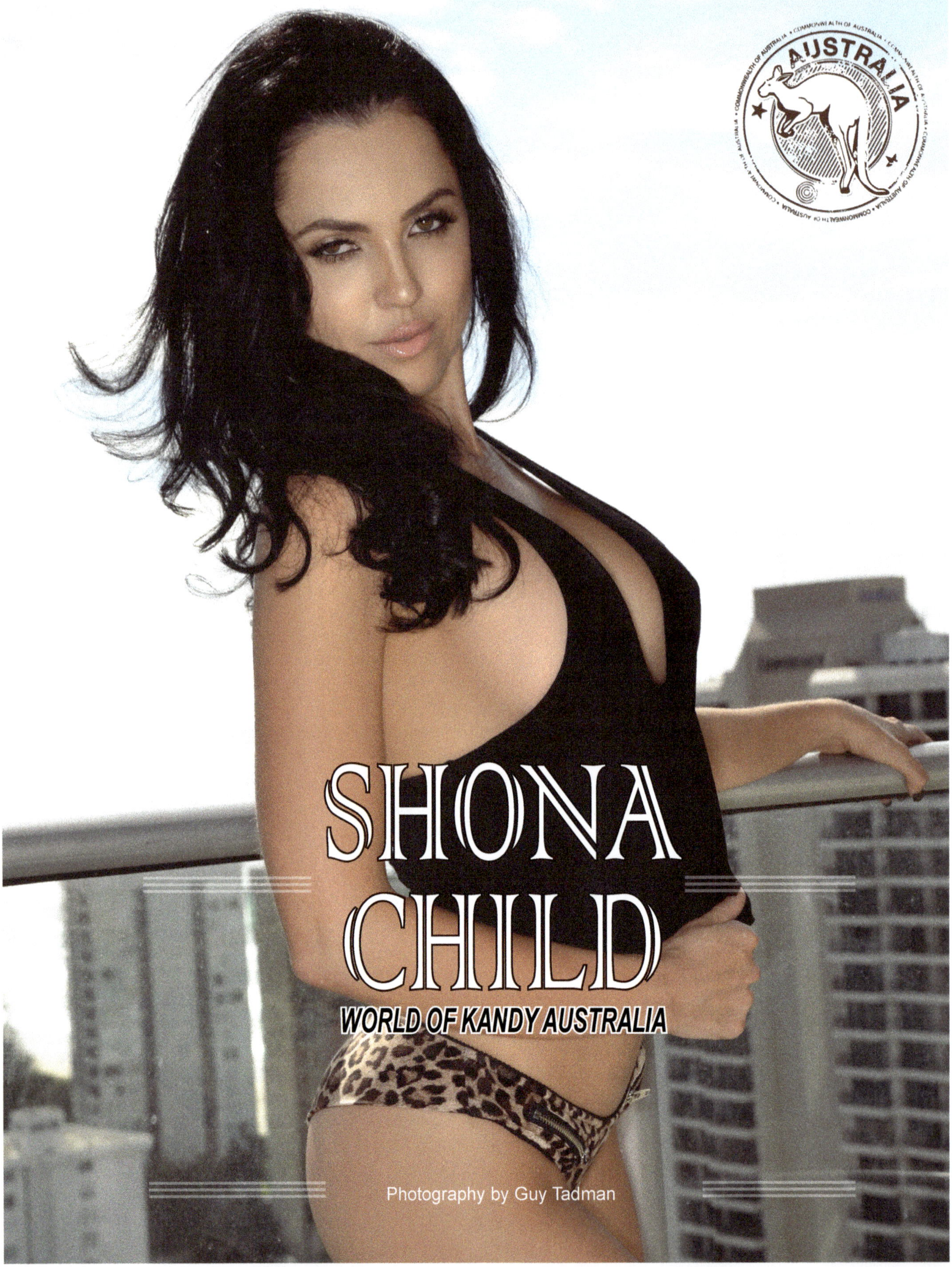

AUSTRALIA
COMMONWEALTH OF AUSTRALIA
SHONA
CHILD
WORLD OF KANDY AUSTRALIA
Photography by Guy Tadman

MY THREE THINGS

What are the 3 Best Things About Australia?
Summer weather, Amazing beaches, Lifestyle

If you were on a deserted island, what are the 3 necessities you require for surviving?
Music, Wine, iPhone

Who are 3 people you would want joining you on a deserted island?
My partner and two closest friends.

Where are the 3 places in the world you have not visited that are at the top of your list to visit?
Cancun, Ibiza, and Vegas for the crazy parties and summer pool events.

KANDY KONCIERGE

Photo credit: fotolia / Kondor83

Ultimate Summer Appetizer
Caliente Bacon Wrapped Shrimp Appetizer
Courtesy Steve Scala

Hey Kandy fans! Sorry for being gone for a bit but your Kandy Koncierge is back and do I have the ultimate outdoor summer appetize for you. It's summertime and time to step up your culinary skills. Show up with these beauties at your next friendly get together and you'll be the talk of the night and the ladies lining up for the main course.

INGREDIENTS

- 1 Pound Bacon I prefer the thick-sliced bacon you can purchase at your local market's butcher counter, absent the hickory smoke or Applewood smoke flavoring.
- 16 to 20 Uncooked Shrimp – If there is a local seafood market run down there and get yourself some fresh, extra jumbo size shrimp. If you don't have a local seafood market, then your local grocery market butcher counter will do.
- ¼ Cup Olive Oil
- 1 Cut Up Lime
- 1 Teaspoon Cayenne Pepper
- 2 Habanero Peppers (Jalapeno if you prefer least heat)
- 2 Cloves Fresh Garlic
- Fresh Rosemary
- Black Olives
- Toothpicks or Wooden Grill Skewers (no metal)

Dice up the habanero peppers and garlic cloves. Slice lime into quarter sections. In a mixing bowl combine olive oil, cayenne, and diced ingredients. Squeeze the juice from the lime into the mixing bowl and give it a quick whisk.

Clean the shrimp. Add the shrimp to the mixing bowl; stir until all the ingredients are coated. Pour the contents of the mixing bowl into an air tight plastic bag and add the cut up pieces of lime. Seal and place in the fridge for 1 hour.

Fire up the coals about 30 minutes prior to the conclusion of the marinade time. Remove the bacon from the package and cut the slices in half.

Remove the marinated shrimp from the fridge. Wrap bacon around each individual shrimp. Place a toothpick through each shrimp to hold the bacon in place or if using grill skewers pierce the shrimp with the skewer, 3 to 4 shrimp per skewer. Pull a sprig of Rosemary and place it in between the shrimp and bacon.

Quickly, whisk the surface of the grill with olive oil so as to reduce the likelihood of the shrimp sticking to the surface of the grill. Use a long, barbeque brush so as to not burn yourself.

Using tongs, gently place the shrimp on to the grill. Grill 5 minutes per side, turning gently with the tongs. The shrimp will appear opaque when done. Remove from grill. Garnish plate with black olives and serve.

Bon a petit!

KANDY FITNESS

FITNESS MYTHS DEBUNKED

WRITTEN BY DAN STEVENS

Hey everyone! As one embarks on their fitness journey, you're likely asking yourself a few questions. And, as a woman they may be one thing and for a man they will be different. Here are a few fitness myths debunked for you.

As a guy, I want to put on lots of muscle. Here's the bottom line. Start eating and I mean a lot! Figure out how many calories you need at rest (Your BMR) and go above and beyond that number for total calorie intake. Eat big to get big! If you find that you aren't growing like you hope, eating in good fat is a good way to get in calories. But always remember, building quality muscle takes a long time.

When I'm in the gym, I exercise in the weight room for at least 2 hours! This is overkill. If you're strictly working on resistance training, less is more. Your goal should be to pump as much blood as possible in the specific muscle. Remember, you aren't training for endurance.

"As a woman, I don't want to lift and become bulky." Ladies! This simply isn't true. It takes years to build muscle and a female's body works primarily with estrogen and not testosterone, making it that much more difficult. So don't worry ladies.

"As a woman, I hear protein will also make me look bulky and is only for men." Wrong! Protein is an essential nutrient in any human's diet. You need it to simply recover from daily activity. You need more to help recover from exercise.

Muscle weighs more than fat. Wrong again! A pound of feathers weighs the same as a pound of pennies. Muscle and fat does not have different weights but rather different densities. So this would explain why if you take two people with the same body weight but one who's muscular versus one who is fatter, they look completely different.

I hope I have shed some light on a few fitness misconceptions and why they don't hold a lot of truth.

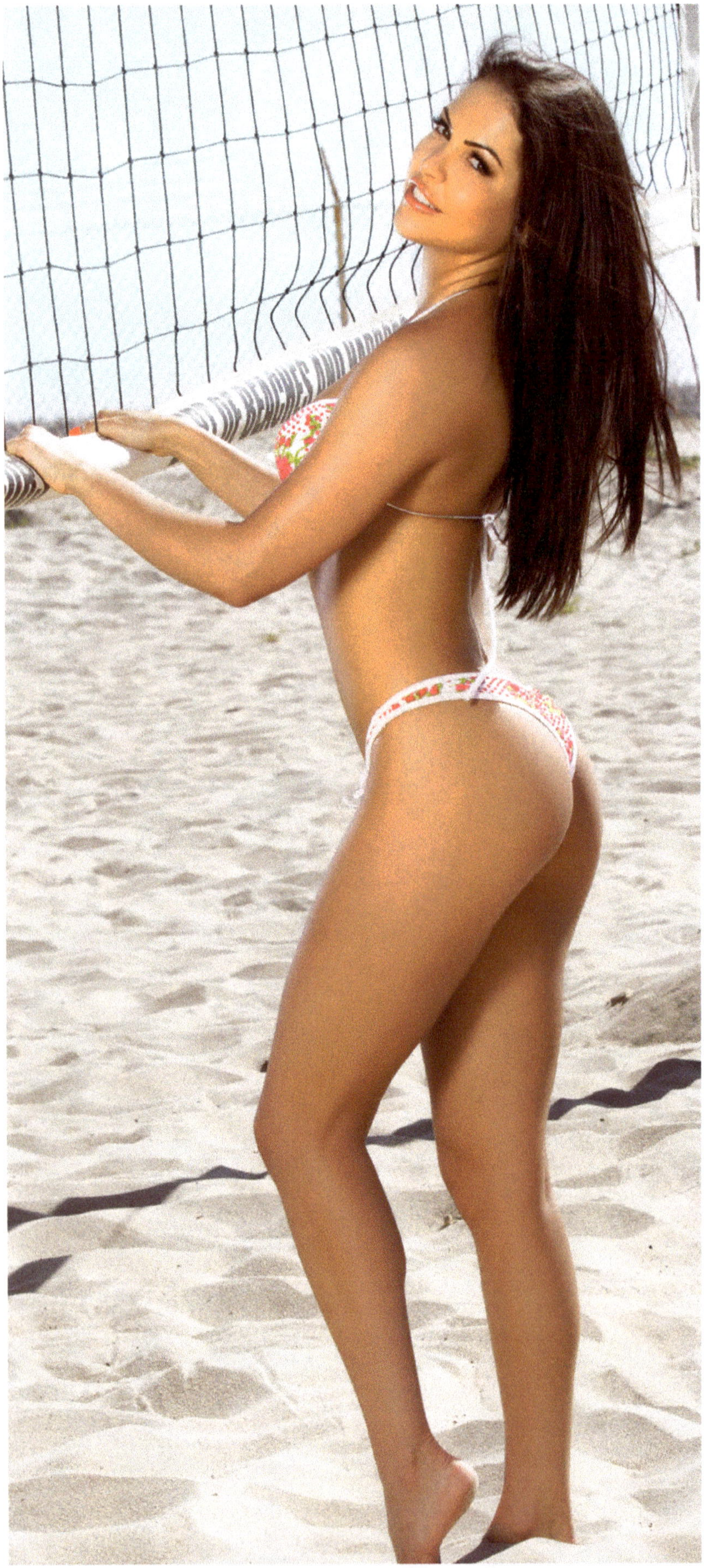

Kandy MAGAZINE

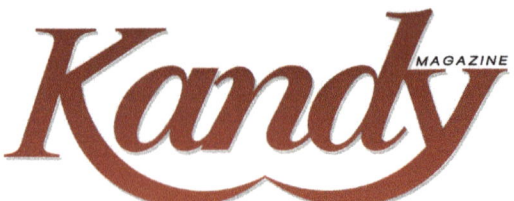

Make payment out to and Mail to:
Kandy Enterprises
7260 W Azure Dr. Ste 140-639
Las Vegas, NV 89130

Yes! I want KANDY! SEND ME:

6 issues for $54 (1 year)
12 issues for $96 (2 Years)
18 issues for $126 (3 Years)

____
First Name

____
Last Name

____
Street Address

____
Street Address

____
City

____
State

____
Zip Code

Remember Payment Enclosed
Please allow 6 to 8 weeks for delivery of first issue.
For Credit card payment options
www.kandy.store

www.ingramcontent.com/pod-product-compliance
Lightning Source LLC
LaVergne TN
LVHW072122060526
838201LV00068B/4954